"You can't take all that, Jerry," said Susan. "There's no room in the car."

"There's also no electricity in the woods," reminded Dad, "but the bug spray is a good idea."

The family loaded the car and began the drive up to Grizzly Lake. "Are we almost there?" asked Jerry and Susan every five minutes.

"We'll let you know," said Mom. "Meanwhile, why don't you play a travel game? Count how many kinds of vehicles you see on the road."

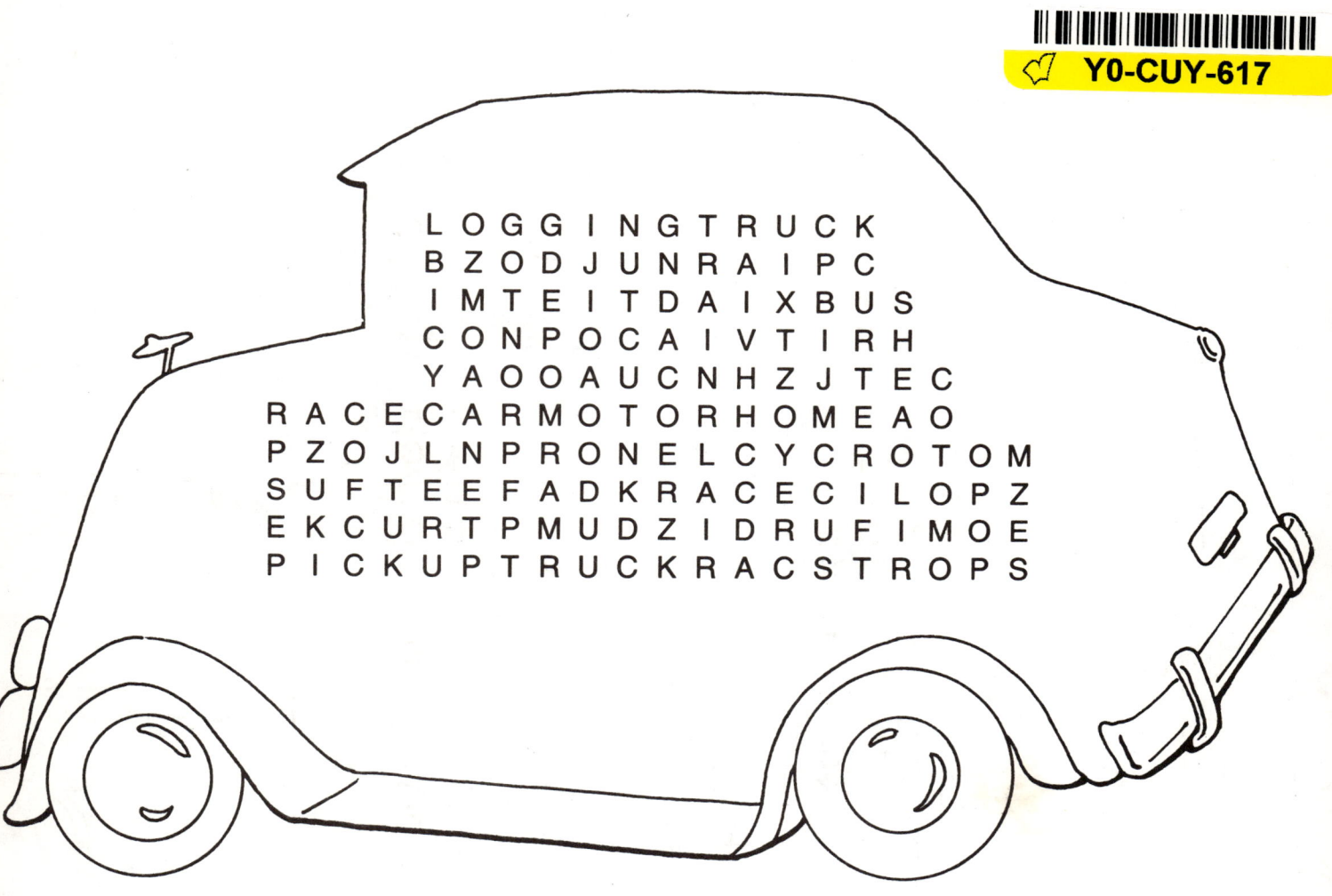

```
        L O G G I N G T R U C K
        B Z O D J U N R A I P C
        I M T E I T D A I X B U S
        C O N P O C A I V T I R H
        Y A O O A U C N H Z J T E C
R A C E C A R M O T O R H O M E A O
P Z O J L N P R O N E L C Y C R O T O M
S U F T E E F A D K R A C E C I L O P Z
E K C U R T P M U D Z I D R U F I M O E
P I C K U P T R U C K R A C S T R O P S
```

Find and circle the vehicles that Jerry and Susan saw.

LOGGING TRUCK	MOTOR HOME	POLICE CAR	RACE CAR	TAXI	VAN
PICKUP TRUCK	DUMP TRUCK	SPORTS CAR	TRAIN	BUS	CAR
MOTORCYCLE	FIRE TRUCK	BICYCLE	CAMPER	MOPED	

Suddenly, Jerry saw a sign. "It says Grizzly Lake is two miles ahead! We're here!" he yelled. Jerry and Susan saw mountains, trees, a dirt road and the edge of a clear lake.

"It doesn't look like anybody has been here before," said Susan. "We're just like Columbus discovering a new place!"

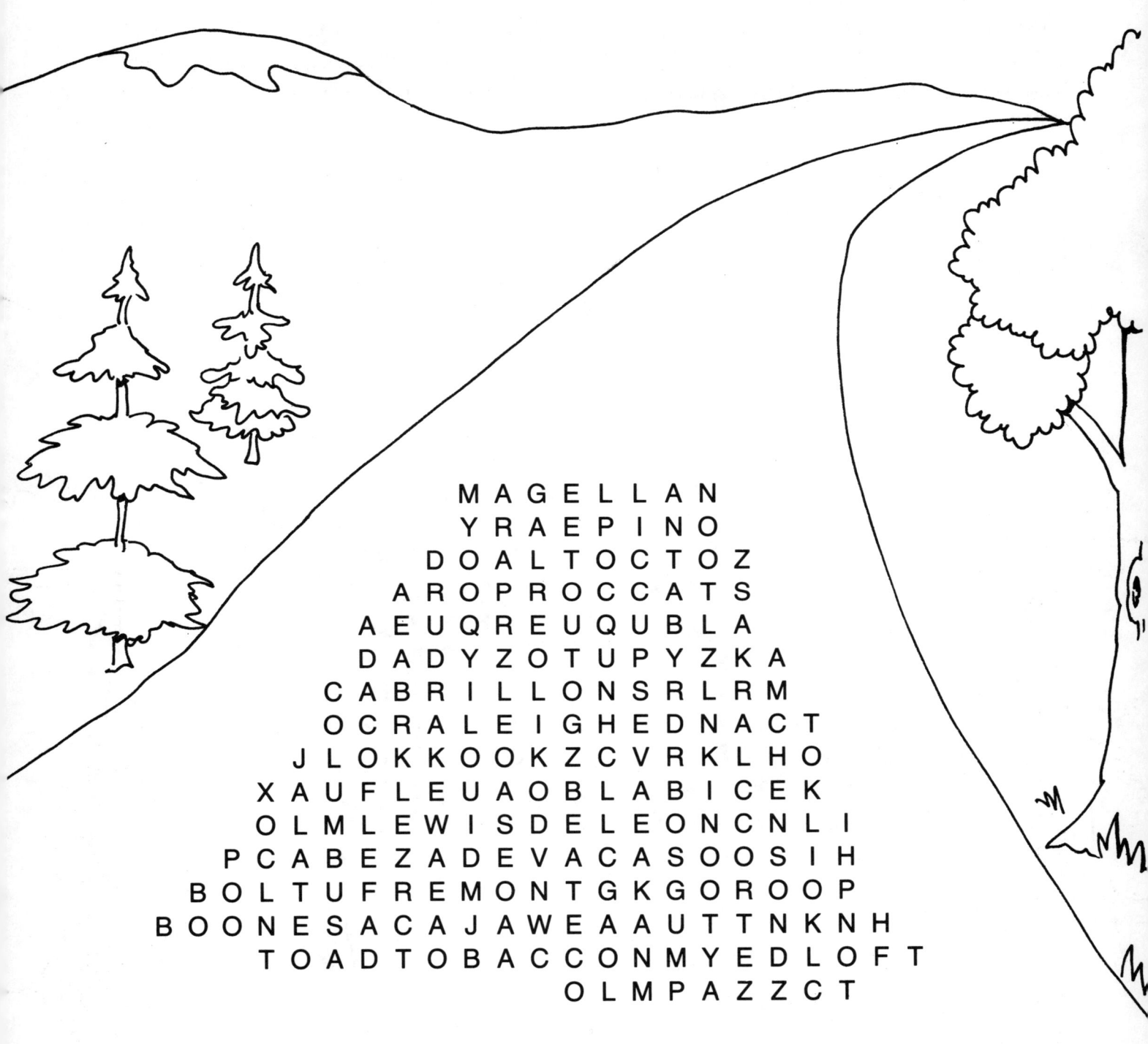

Find and circle the names of explorers.

RALEIGH	COLUMBUS	CABEZA DE VACA	ERICSON	PEARY	BYRD
BOONE	SACAJAWEA	ALBUQUERQUE	DE LEON	CLARK	CABOT
BALBOA	MAGELLAN	DA GAMA	FREMONT	LEWIS	DRAKE
CORTEZ	VESPUCCI	CABRILLO	HENSON		

9

Dad parked the car. "Put on your backpacks, everybody," said Mom.

"Backpacks?" asked Susan. "Why do we need backpacks?"

"We have to hike five miles to find a good campsite. This side of the lake isn't good for fishing."

Susan and Jerry groaned and strapped on their backpacks. "This is heavy," said Jerry.

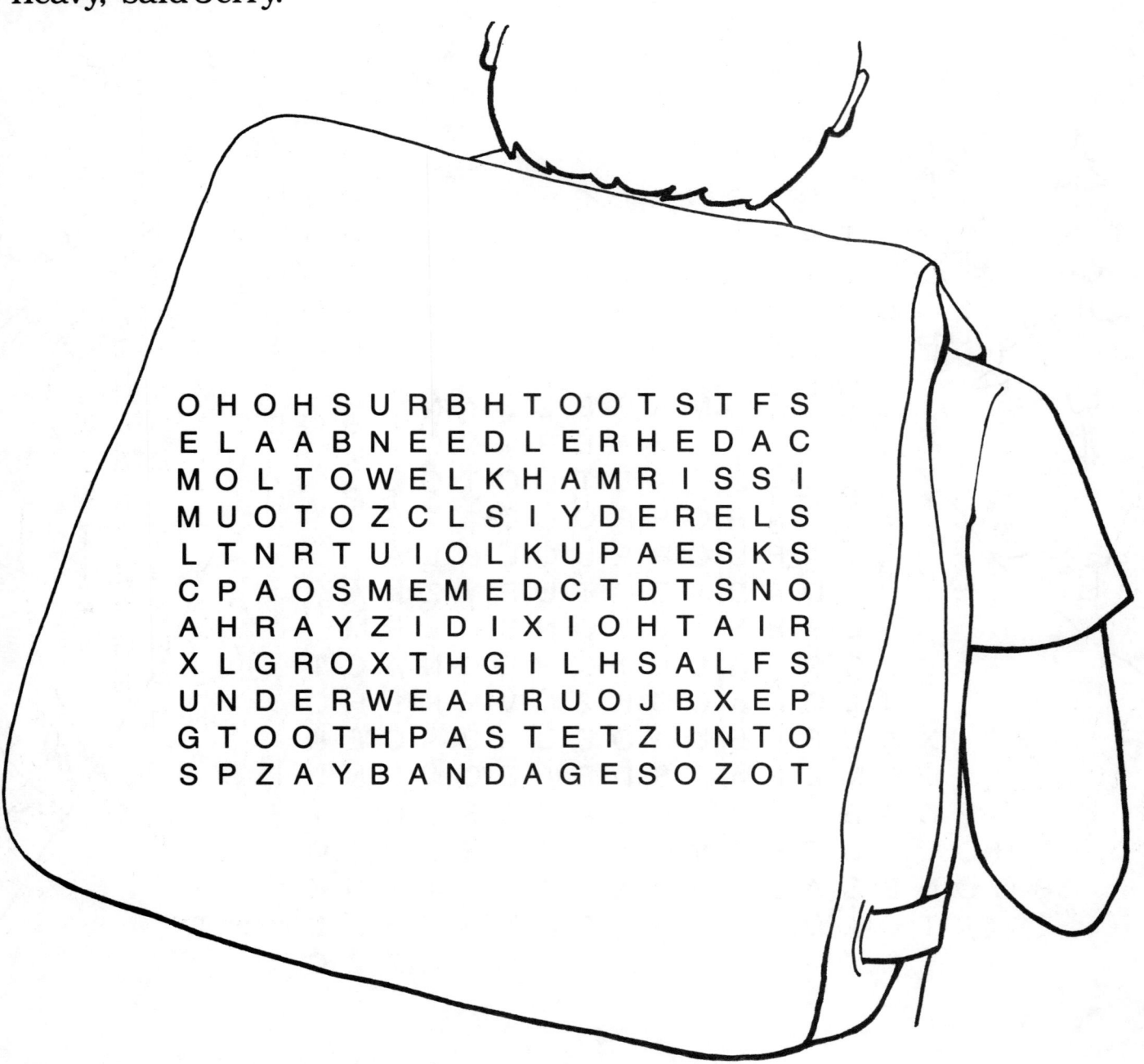

```
O H O H S U R B H T O O T S T F S
E L A A B N E E D L E R H E D A C
M O L T O W E L K H A M R I S S I
M U O T O Z C L S I Y D E R E L S
L T N R T U I O L K U P A E S K S
C P A O S M E M E D C T D T S N O
A H R A Y Z I D I X I O H T A I R
X L G R O X T H G I L H S A L F S
U N D E R W E A R R U O J B X E P
G T O O T H P A S T E T Z U N T O
S P Z A Y B A N D A G E S O Z O T
```

Find and circle everything that Susan and Jerry have in their backpacks.

TOOTHBRUSH	SOCKS	TOWEL	GRANOLA	THREAD
UNDERWEAR	HAT	TOOTHPASTE	DRY MILK	NEEDLE
BOOTS	SOAP	BATTERIES	BANDAGES	
FLASHLIGHT	KNIFE	TRAIL MIX	SCISSORS	

10

They walked and walked and walked. "It's beautiful here," said Susan. "Maybe camping isn't so bad after all."

But Jerry still complained. "Yes it is! My feet hurt. I'm going to rest here for a minute." Jerry sat down. Then he jumped up fast! "Ants! I sat on red ants. Wait for me!"

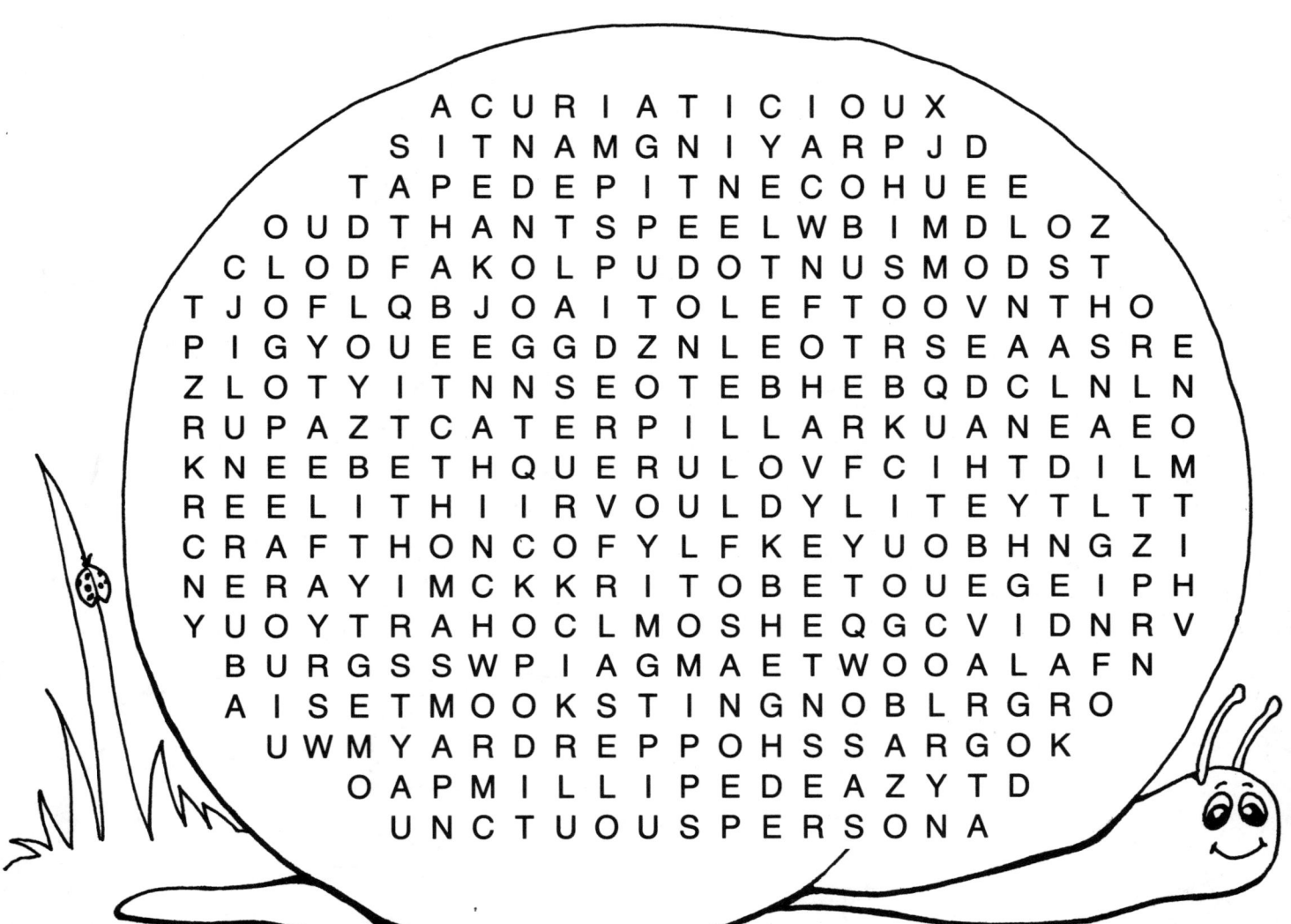

There are lots of crawling, buzzing, flying creatures in the woods. Find and circle them.

GNAT	BEE	GRASSHOPPER	CENTIPEDE	SNAIL
TICK	ANT	CATERPILLAR	INCHWORM	SPIDER
MOTH	FLY	PRAYING MANTIS	MILLIPEDE	BEETLE
GRUB	FLEA	MOSQUITO	BUTTERFLY	LADYBUG

"Let's camp here," said Mom, as they walked through some trees to a clearing. "This is a good spot." Mom and Dad showed Jerry and Susan how to clean up the campsite they chose.

"We can pitch the tent now," said Dad. He got out the pegs and the tent.

"I can do it!" said Jerry. He drove the pegs into the ground.

12

Susan ran into the tent as soon as it was up.
"Oh no!" she yelled, as the whole tent fell on her.
"You're not supposed to stand up in a tent if it's shorter than you," said Jerry. "I'll help you put it back up, Susan."
"You two are becoming real campers," said Dad. Susan and Jerry smiled.

"Let's go exploring," said Susan.

"That's a good idea!" said Jerry. Mom and Dad told them not to get lost.

"Leave markers on trees so you'll know the trail," said Dad. "You can use this chalk." Jerry and Susan started out. They saw many kinds of trees on the way.

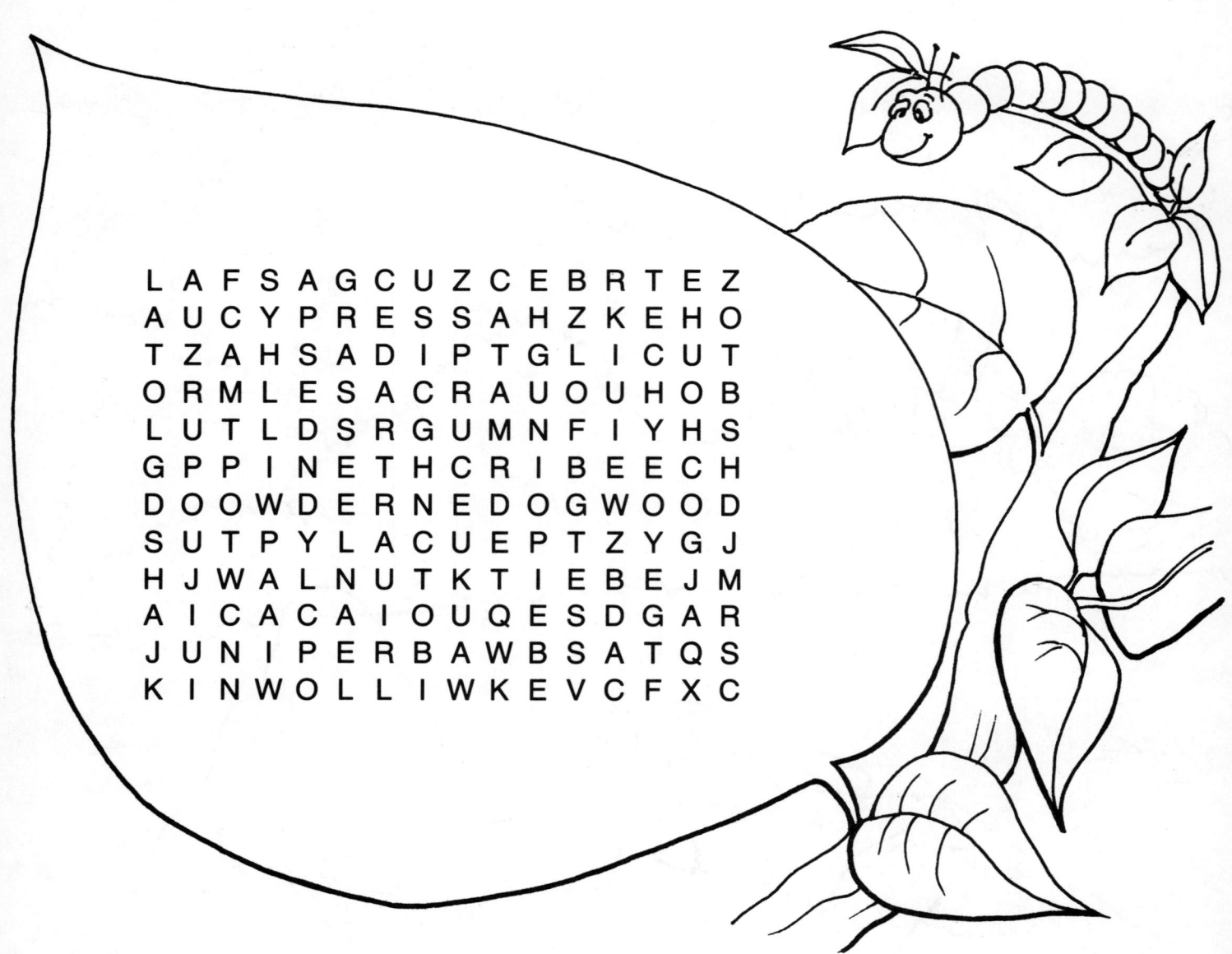

Find and circle the kinds of trees Susan and Jerry found in the woods.

REDWOOD	ALDER	SEQUOIA	PINE	WALNUT
EUCALYPTUS	BIRCH	DOGWOOD	ELM	WILLOW
CHESTNUT	CEDAR	JUNIPER	GUM	CYPRESS
ACACIA	BEECH	POPLAR	OAK	SPRUCE

Jerry and Susan walked around the lake. "Do you think there are really grizzly bears here?" asked Susan.

"I hope not," said Jerry. "Listen! What's that noise? Look out!" A small tree came crashing to the ground. Jerry and Susan walked toward the noise.

"It's a beaver!" Jerry yelled. The beaver looked at Jerry and Susan. It started to chomp on branches from the little tree.

"It doesn't look very dangerous," Susan teased Jerry. The beaver took its branch and waddled away.

"I think I like beavers," said Jerry. "Let's go back. It must be time for dinner."

"What's that smell?" asked Susan, as she and Jerry ran toward the campsite.

"Hot dogs!" said Mom. "We got the whole campsite ready while you were gone. How was your trip? Did you run into any animals?"

"We had fun," said Jerry. "We saw a beaver, but that's all. I don't think there are many animals around here."

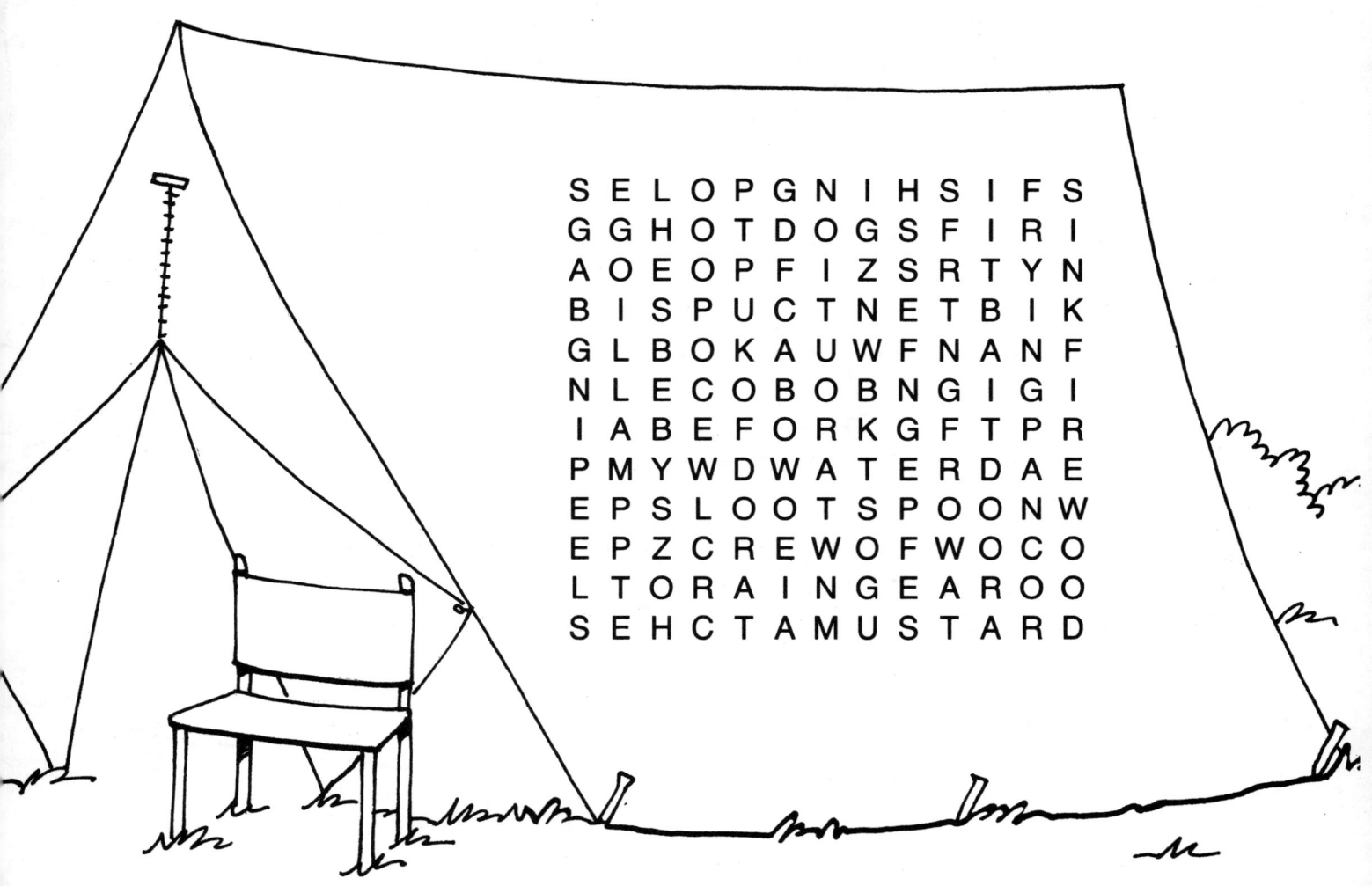

```
S E L O P G N I H S I F S
G G H O T D O G S F I R I
A O E O P F I Z S R T Y N
B I S P U C T N E T B I K
G L B O K A U W F N A N F
N L E C O B O B N G I G I
I A B E F O R K G F T P R
P M Y W D W A T E R D A E
E P S L O O T S P O O N W
E P Z C R E W O F W O C O
L T O R A I N G E A R O O
S E H C T A M U S T A R D
```

Find and circle all the things at the campsite.

PEG	FRYING PAN	HOT DOG	MUSTARD	TENT	MATCHES	RAIN GEAR
CUP	FISHING POLE	FIREWOOD	KNIFE	FORK	STOOL	
BUN	SLEEPING BAG	OIL LAMP	WATER	BAIT	SPOON	

"Let's sing camp songs," said Jerry. Dad taught them the songs he used to sing when he was a little boy.

Mom put out the fire. "Time for bed," said Mom.

"But it's dark," said Susan. "There's no night light."

"I'll protect you," said Jerry. "Don't be afraid." They said good night and got into their sleeping bags.

"Whooooo! Whooooo!" came the sound from out of the darkness.

"Wh-wh-what's that?" asked Jerry.

"I think it's just an owl," said Susan. "But I'm not afraid, because you're going to protect me," she smiled.

Jerry and Susan fell fast asleep, but Jerry dreamed all night about strange things in the woods.

```
P O T M U B I G F O O T O A D P D D O Z O T
O P O S E U W I O J O A F L M A R O V R E N
L D R L T S O H G B A B U J O R A N E G A E
T A E K O W L J U M L K W Z N K C U R E T P
E V A C U J F K U F D I N O S A U R O R L R
R Q E I S T Z M O T T Y N M T M L I W F A E
U C M S T Q M L D C J A C B E L A D I U Q S
R D K T A Y B I H T H O M I R A K T S A U A
G F L O W E R E W I E N O E T A B B Y S I E
E R I P M A V N I E T S N E K N A R F I D S
```

Find and circle all the scary things that Jerry dreamed about.

GHOST	MUMMY	WEREWOLF	OWL	ZOMBIE
GOBLIN	FRANKENSTEIN	MONSTER	BAT	BIGFOOT
CAVE	SEA SERPENT	DRACULA	WOLF	WITCH
SQUID	DINOSAUR	VAMPIRE	FOG	

19

"Good morning!" said Susan. "I slept great! How about you?"
"Me, too," said Jerry, "sort of."
"Is breakfast ready?" Jerry asked Mom and Dad.
"You have to catch your own," laughed Mom. "Here are the poles. There is the lake. Dig up some worms for bait and you'll be ready!"

"I'm hungry," said Jerry, as he and Susan dug for worms. They filled a whole can full of them with no trouble at all.

"They're so squishy," said Jerry. "Now we have to bait the hook with them. Eeeeoooo!"

Or else we don't get to eat," frowned Susan. "I wonder what kinds of fish we can catch here. There are lots of different freshwater fish."

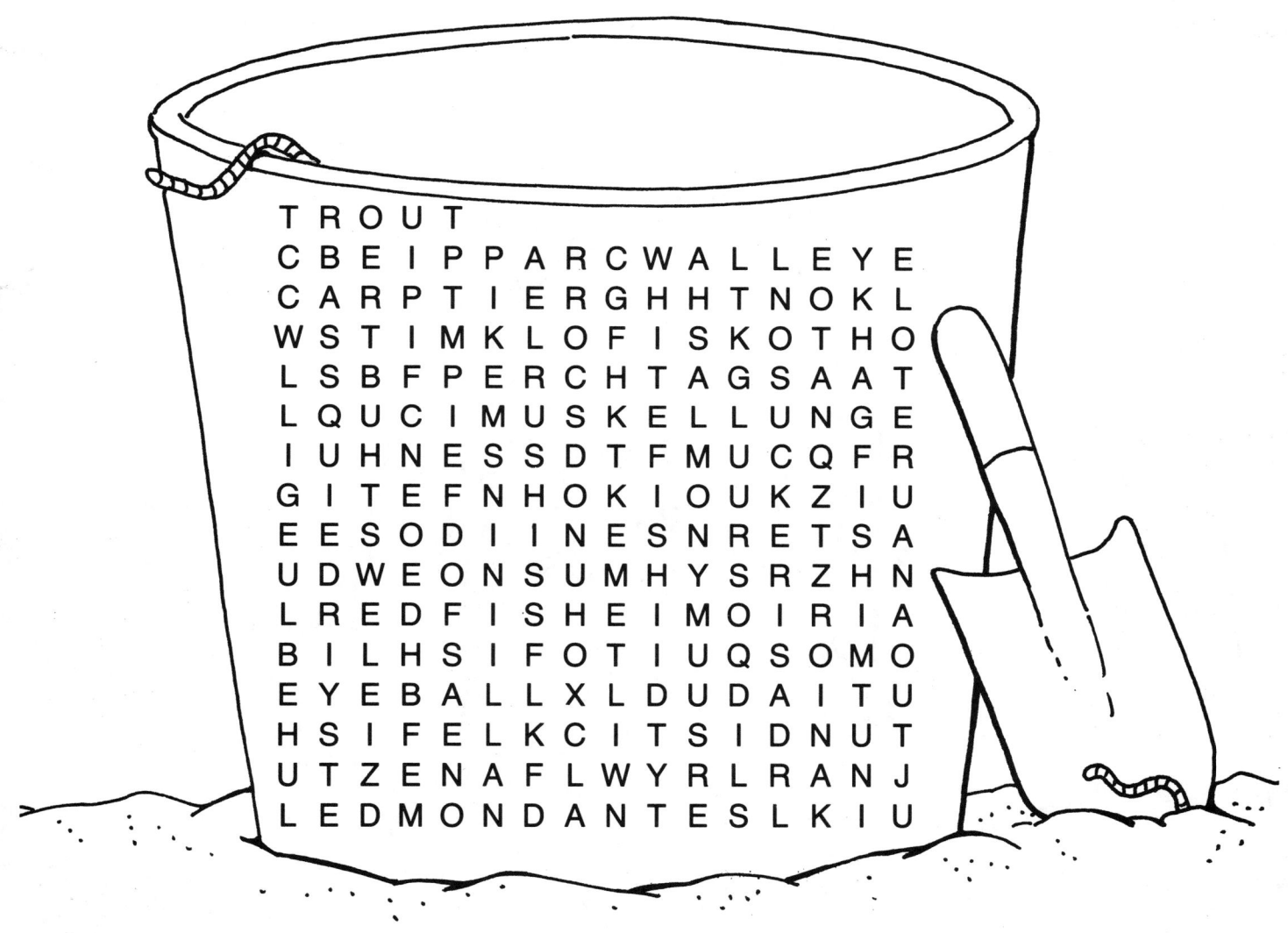

Find and circle the kinds of freshwater fish.

CATFISH	MUSKELLUNGE	TROUT	WHITEFISH	BASS	SUNFISH
REDFISH	STICKLEFISH	PERCH	BLUEGILL	PIKE	HAGFISH
SALMON	MOSQUITO FISH	SUCKER	WALLEYE	CARP	CRAPPIE

"I caught one! I caught one!" yelled Susan. She reeled in a big catfish. "Look at his whiskers!" said Jerry. Suddenly, he felt a pull on his line. "I got one, too!" Jerry pulled and pulled. Susan helped. "Here it comes!" yelled Jerry. "Oh no, it's just a big fisherman's boot full of water." Jerry turned the boot upside down. Out fell a trout!

Jerry and Susan went back to the campsite with their catch. Mom and Dad cooked the fish.

"This tastes better than Floaty-Oaty cereal," declared Susan. "We should catch our breakfast every day. How do you like camping out now, Jerry?"

"I like it a lot!" he answered, as he wiped his mouth. "It's better than anything we do for fun at home."

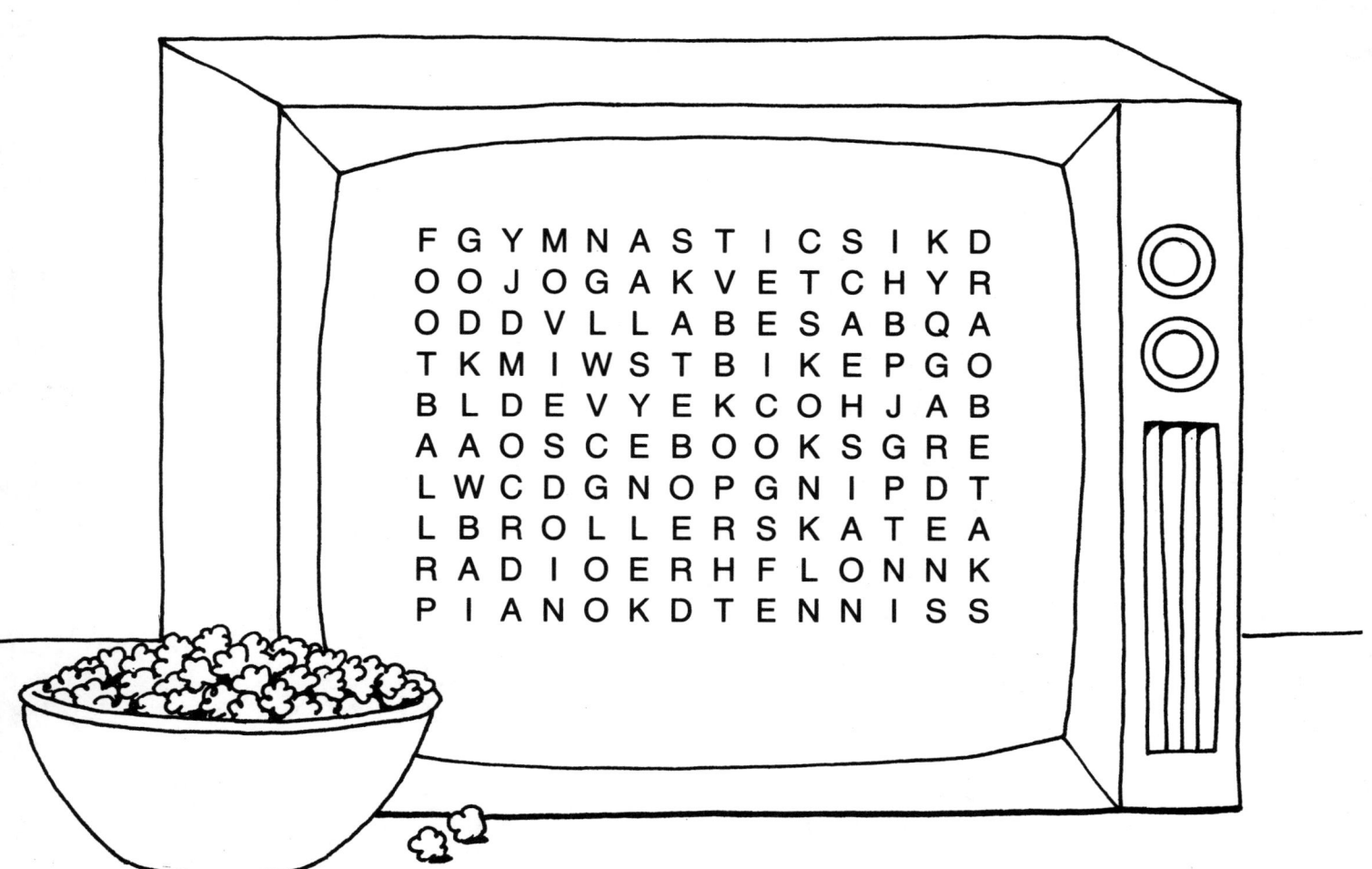

Find and circle the things that Jerry and Susan do at home.

BIKE	ROLLERSKATE	TV	FOOTBALL	TENNIS
RADIO	SKATEBOARD	DIVE	BASEBALL	MOVIES
SWIM	GYMNASTICS	JOG	WALK DOG	GARDEN
BOOKS	PING PONG	COOK	HOCKEY	PIANO

"Let's clean the campsite, then we'll go exploring again," said Jerry. "We can go on a different path this time."

"We're such good campers, we don't even need to mark our trail," said Susan. Jerry agreed.

"Be back soon," said Mom and Dad. Jerry and Susan set out.

"This is a good path," said Susan. "I'm going to pick up interesting things and put them in my backpack."

"I'll help you," said Jerry, "but let's be careful about what we pick up. We don't want to pick up poison ivy or poison oak!"

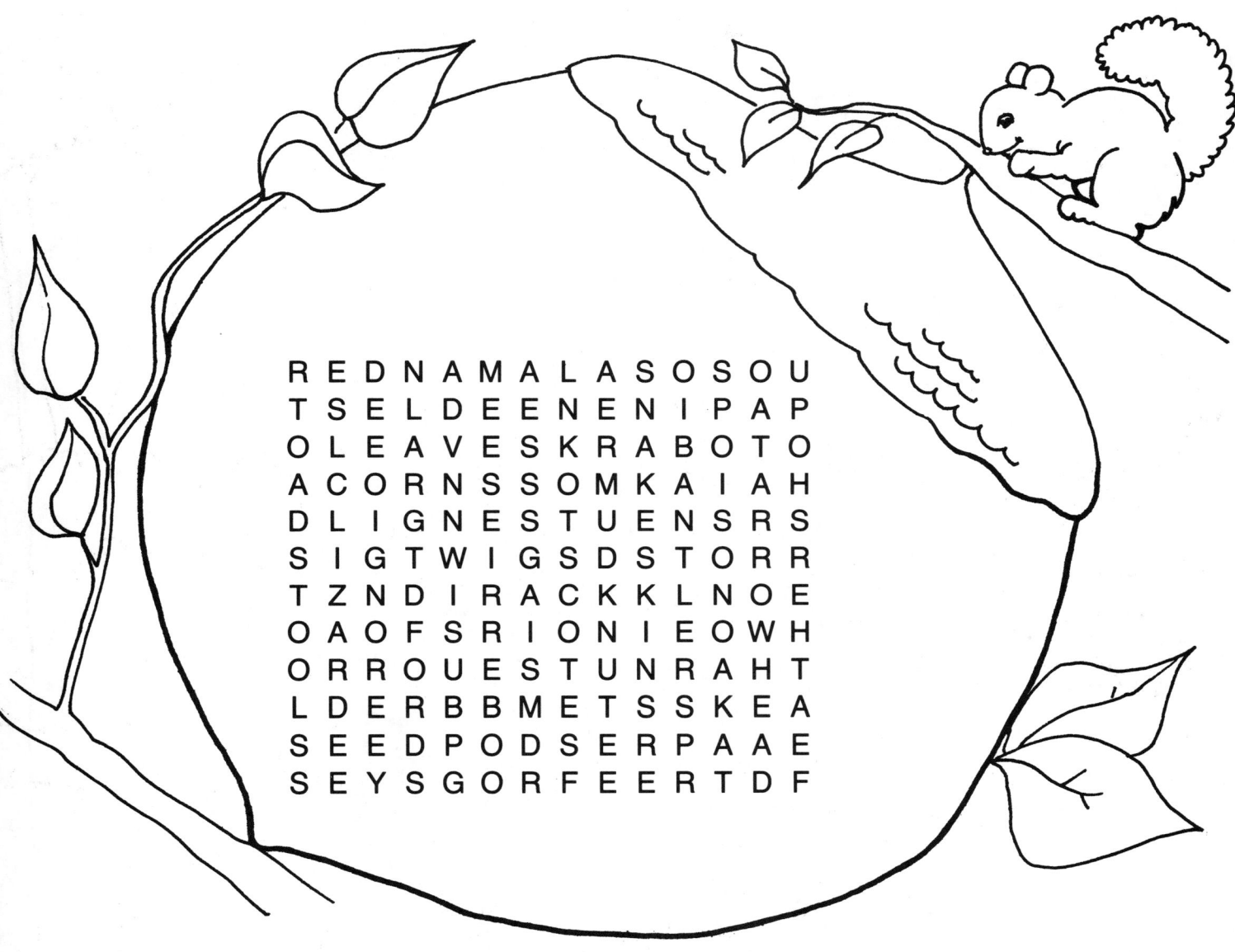

```
R E D N A M A L A S O S O U
T S E L D E E N E N I P A P
O L E A V E S K R A B O T O
A C O R N S S O M K A I A H
D L I G N E S T U E N S R S
S I G T W I G S D S T O R R
T Z N D I R A C K K L N O E
O A O F S R I O N I E O W H
O R R O U E S T U N R A H T
L D E R B B M E T S S K E A
S E E D P O D S E R P A A E
S E Y S G O R F E E R T D F
```

Find and circle everything that Susan and Jerry found in the woods.

SALAMANDER	SNAKESKIN	ANTLERS	ACORN	MOSS
TOADSTOOL	TREE FROG	BERRIES	NEST	TWIG
ARROWHEAD	FEATHER	LIZARD	NUT	BARK
POISON OAK	SEED POD	LEAVES	MUD	LOG
PINE NEEDLES				

"Let's go back," said Jerry. He and Susan turned around. "Hey! Where did the path go?"

"It must be around here somewhere," said Susan. They looked all around.

There was no path. "We didn't mark the trees this time," groaned Jerry.

"I'm hungry," said Susan. "Let's have a snack. Then we'll be able to think better."

"Good idea," said Jerry. "What did you bring?"

"Me?" asked Susan. "I emptied my backpack so I could fill it with the things we found in the woods. What did you bring?"

"Nothing," said Jerry. "Just some comics. I thought I could read them while we ate the snacks that I thought you were bringing! I'm starving!"

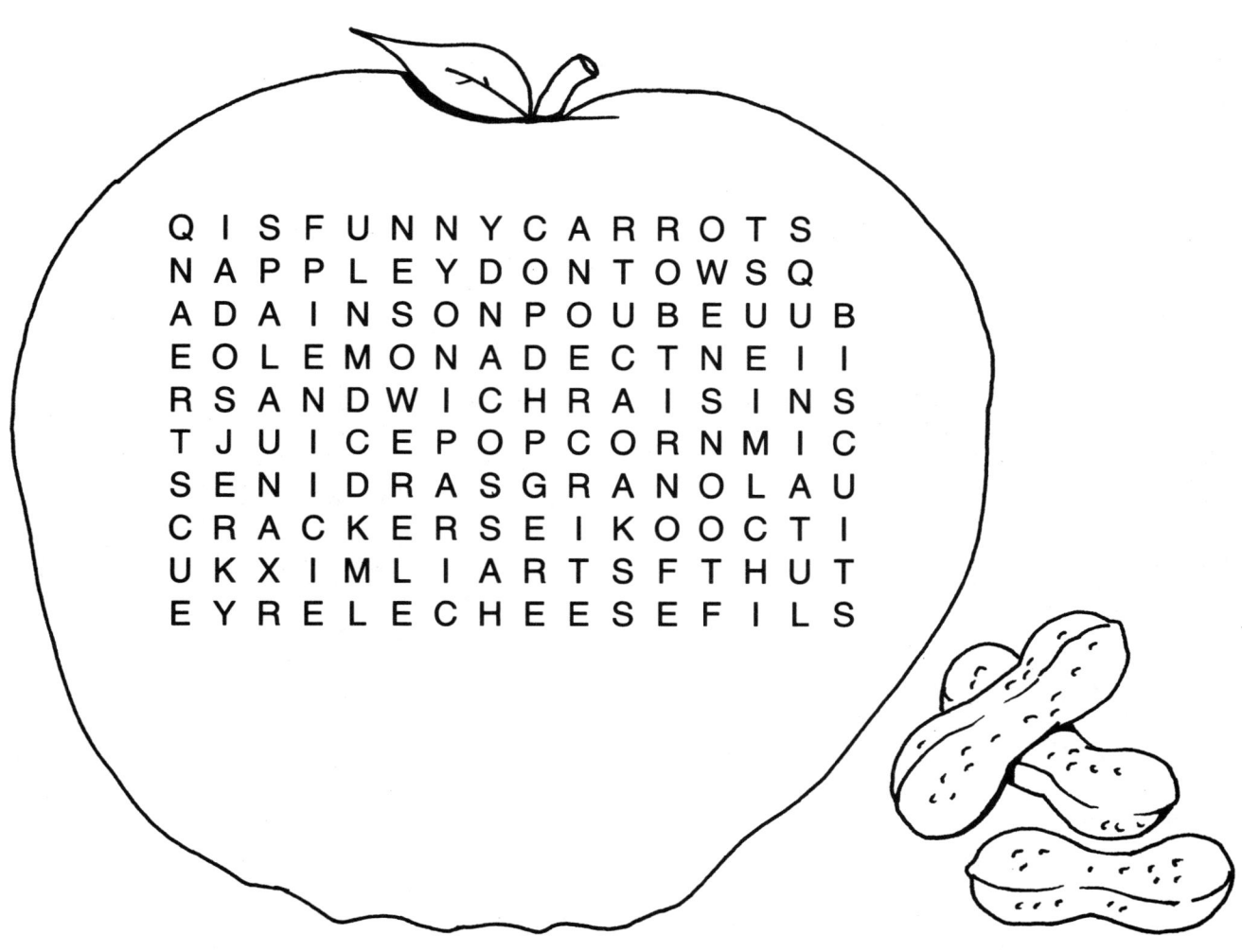

```
Q I S F U N N Y C A R R O T S
N A P P L E Y D O N T O W S Q
A D A I N S O N P O U B E U U B
E O L E M O N A D E C T N E I I
R S A N D W I C H R A I S I N S
T J U I C E P O P C O R N M I C
S E N I D R A S G R A N O L A U
C R A C K E R S E I K O O C T I
U K X I M L I A R T S F T H U T
E Y R E L E C H E E S E F I L S
```

Find and circle snacks that Jerry and Susan could have brought.

TRAIL MIX	CANDY	POPCORN	NUTS	RAISINS
LEMONADE	CELERY	CRACKERS	PEAR	COOKIES
SANDWICH	APPLE	CARROTS	SODA	CHEESE
SARDINES	JUICE	GRANOLA	JERKY	BISCUITS

"We should have marked the trees. We have the chalk. Maybe we can leave a message on some of the trees," suggested Susan.

"That's a good idea," said Jerry, calming down. They walked and marked the trees, "Follow these trees to find two lost kids."

Jerry and Susan kept walking. "I think I see a clearing up ahead," said Jerry. He and Susan started to run toward the clearing.

"Yow!" screamed Jerry, as he came to a screeching stop. "It's a cliff!"

They both looked down. Sure enough, it was a steep cliff. And Jerry had stopped just in time!

"Now I really need something to eat," said Jerry. "Being scared always makes me hungry."

"There's a big hill up ahead," said Susan. "I bet we could climb it and see our campsite from the top."

"Hill?" shouted Jerry. "That's a mountain. It looks as big as Mount Everest!"

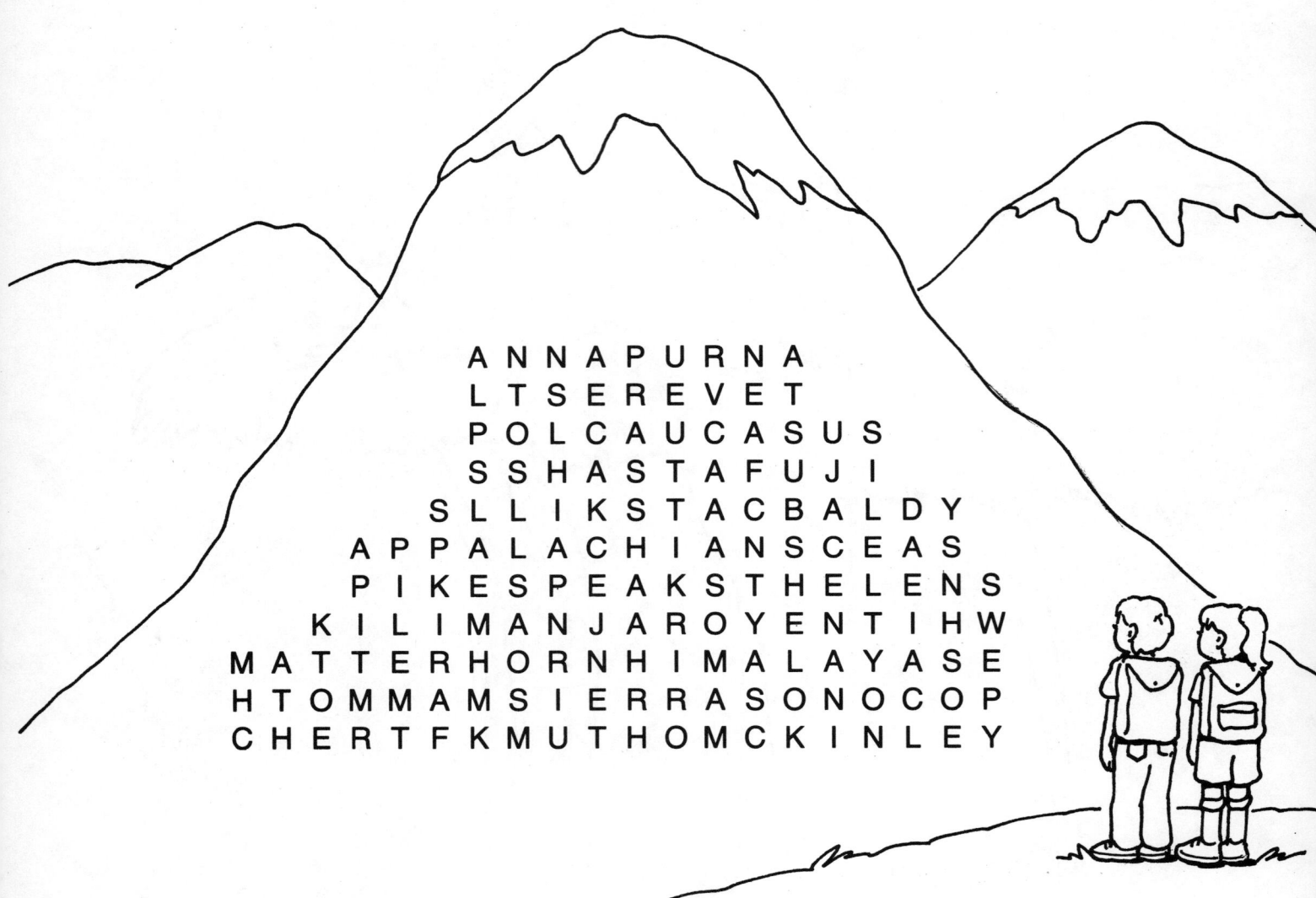

Find and circle the names of mountains and mountain ranges.

EVEREST	APPALACHIANS	PIKE'S PEAK	FUJI	MCKINLEY
POCONOS	KILIMANJARO	ANNAPURNA	SHASTA	MAMMOTH
SIERRAS	MATTERHORN	CAUCASUS	ATLAS	CATSKILLS
BALDY	HIMALAYAS	ST. HELENS	ALPS	WHITNEY

"Let's just go back in the woods," said Jerry. "Maybe some of the trees we passed will look familiar." They continued walking in the woods.

"We're just like Hansel and Gretel," sniffed Susan. "All we need now is a witch's house!"

"But don't forget, that story had a happy ending," said Jerry. "Most fairy tales do."

Find and circle the names of characters in fairy tales.

BEAUTY	RED RIDING HOOD	CINDERELLA	THREE PIGS	GRETEL
QUEEN	STEPMOTHER	RAPUNZEL	GRANDMA	WITCH
WOLF	SLEEPING BEAUTY	STEPSISTER	PETER PAN	PRINCE
BEAST	SNOW WHITE	PINOCCHIO	HANSEL	DWARFS

"You know," said Susan, "I found a couple of arrowheads way back there. Maybe there are Indians in these woods. They can show us the way back."

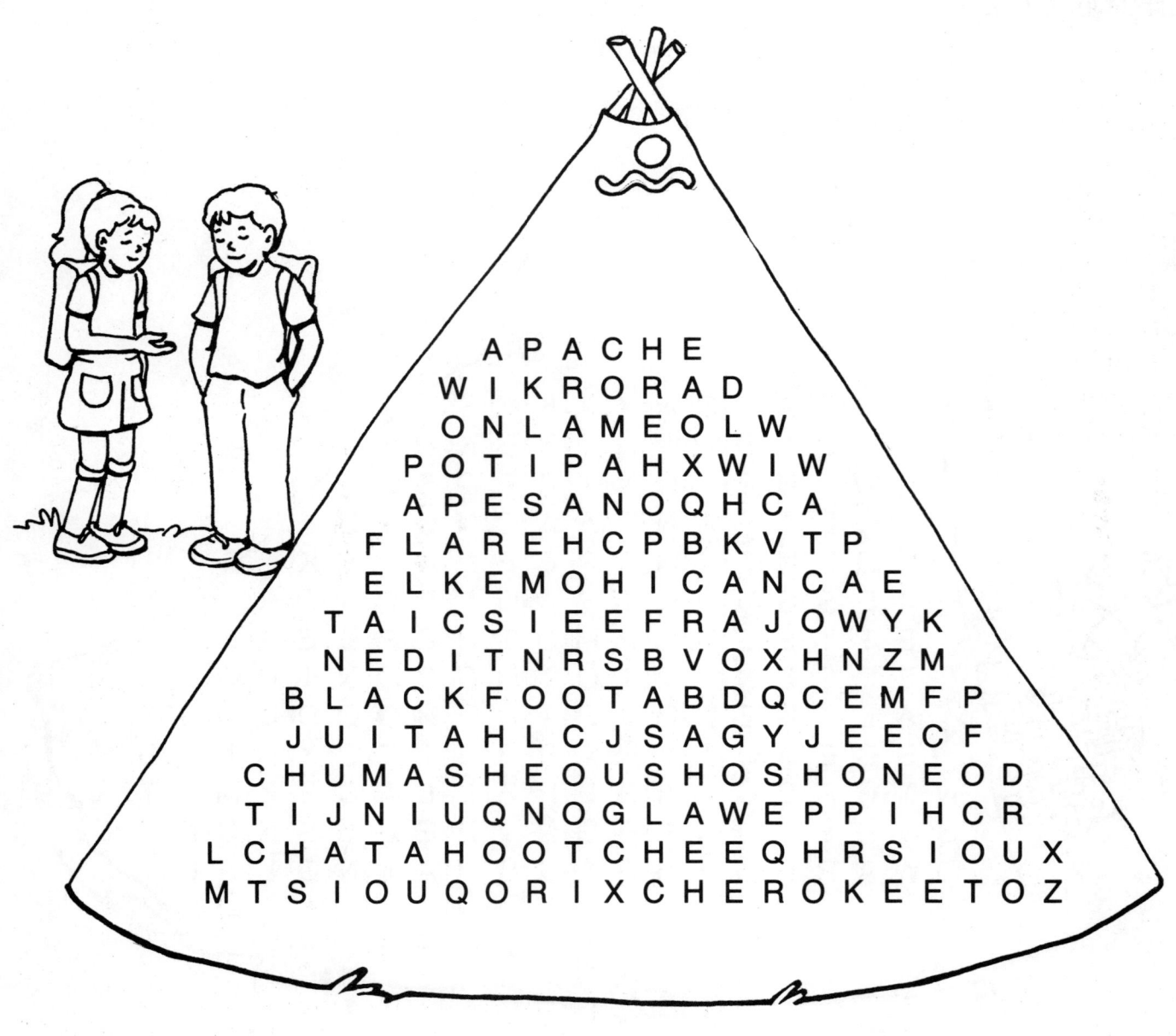

Find and circle the names of Indian tribes.

MOHICAN	ALGONQUIN	APACHE	KICKAPOO	ARAPAHO
BLACKFOOT	CHIPPEWA	SIOUX	CHUMASH	CHEROKEE
SEMINOLE	SHOSHONE	CROW	COMANCHE	PAWNEE
NAVAJO	CHATAHOOTCHEE	HOPI	IROQUOIS	CHOCTAW

Suddenly, they heard the sound of cracking twigs on the ground.
"Don't turn around," said Jerry. "Just keep walking."
But Susan did look behind her, and screamed, "A bear! A bear!"

"Wait!" the bear called out to them. "I've been looking for you."
"Bears don't talk!" said Jerry. The bear lumbered over to the kids. "I heard you talking," he said, "and I read your messages on the trees. That was pretty smart!"

Find and circle things that have to do with bears.

CLAWS	HIBERNATE	POLAR	GRIZZLY	HONEY	CAVE	SLEEP
WOODS	TREE CLIMBING	FISH	KODIAK	TEETH	FUR	STREAM
PAWS	LUMBERING	CUBS	BROWN	GROWL	DEN	BLACK

34

The "bear" took off his head and they saw it was only a man in a bear costume. "You were right," he said. "There are Indians here. We meet here once a year and have our powwow. I always play the great bear. I'm a good tracker, and you kids weren't too hard to find. I'm sorry I scared you. Would you like to come to the powwow?"

Find and circle things that have to do with Indians.

SMOKE SIGNAL	BOW	WIGWAM	FISHING	ARROW
TOMAHAWK	CHIEF	BUFFALO	FOREST	HOGAN
POWWOW	SCOUT	PAPOOSE	TOTEM	TEPEE
KACHINAS	HORSE	HUNTING	FEATHERS	BRAVE

Susan and Jerry went to the powwow. There was singing, dancing and the telling of Indian legends.

"I think we'd better take you back to your campsite now," said John Swiftrunner, the "bear" who had found them. "I'm sure I know where it is." Jerry and Susan said good-bye to everybody and thanked them.

"Now, keep your eyes open," said John. "You'll see lots of interesting things on the way back."

```
A C W A T E R F A L L D A Z R
S L L I H S S A R G E C S O E
T N P I L O X E N T A C K T E
R R A O F D O M U E V A C B S
E S G K O F F J A S E B O U N
A S N D E E R L C A S I R Z I
M E T O R E H P O G H N E Z F
L H K R Z R U E R W E J D Y T
E S T C E S N I N E E O I D O
A U G T O E J G F N T R P U N
F B D I L K S C D T C G S C K
```

Find and circle everything that the kids saw.

GRASS HILL	GOPHER	SNAKE	CAVE	FOX
WILDFLOWER	INSECT	CLIFF	DEER	LOG
WATERFALL	STREAM	ACORN	LEAF	TREE
SPIDER	CABIN	ROCK	BUSH	

"Are you having fun camping?" asked John.

"We sure are!" said Susan. "The mountains are pretty. The lake has lots of great fish in it, we got lost and found, and we met you and your friends!"

"And sleeping outside is fun!" added Jerry. "But I wish we knew the names of all the birds we've seen."

"I'll point them out and tell you about them," said John. "There are many in these woods."

```
Z H V U L T U R E N E D L
O O A G R O U S E E D G I
T P E W L W O R T V S D O
S R V L K H O Z I A E U O O
W O O D P E C K E R L C P L S
A M D B N E Q U A I L K S K Y E Y
L H F L I C K E R P O A R W E L L
L A U G H N B L U E J A Y I M G P
O H U M M I N G B I R D K M R A O
W O R R A P S W A R B L E R E E V
E K L L I W R O O P P I H W N O S
```

Find and circle the birds that live around Grizzly Lake.

OWL	HUMMINGBIRD	SPARROW	BLUEJAY	ROBIN
DUCK	WOODPECKER	SWALLOW	FLICKER	QUAIL
GOOSE	WHIPPOORWILL	TOWHEE	RAVEN	HAWK
DOVE	VULTURE	WARBLER	GROUSE	EAGLE

37

John Swiftrunner and the kids went down, down, down the mountain and around the lake. He showed them many things they had missed while they were upset about being lost.

"I think we should go camping every weekend," said Susan.

"I think we should live here!" said Jerry.

John laughed. "The lake can be a special place to come to as a treat."

"It's okay to get lost if you get found, too," said Jerry. "I wouldn't like to be out here alone. What could I eat?"

"The woods, lake and mountains are full of wild treats to eat," said John. "If you knew what to look for, you'd find good food that is safe to eat."

```
D J A S T U M D E E W E S R O H E
T A C M E S Q U I T E D U L B M L
T N J U N I P E R J O U S T L A P
A O N S H U H S I D A R I Y A Y P
I N M T S H E D S H O E F R C R A
L I O A I K S A F A E S H R K R B
M O O R T W U N B V R R Y E B E A
C N T D F I T D R J U O A B E B R
R S M O R E L E O O M H H E R K C
U J D E E W K L I M C U O U R C D
B M A L L O W I O K R A I L Y A O
A P T L E N R O H T K C U B X H E
H I C K O R Y N U T S H O T S D W
```

Find and circle wild things that are safe and good to eat.

TOMATILLO	MUSTARD	HICKORY NUTS	ACORNS	HORSEWEED
BLACKBERRY	MALLOW	BUCKTHORN	JUNIPER	
DANDELION	MESQUITE	HACKBERRY	ONION	
BLUEBERRY	MILKWEED	CRABAPPLE	MOREL	

"We saw some cabins," said Jerry. "Do some people live here all the time?"

"Yes, some people do," said John.

"I bet this was a great place in the old days," said Susan.

"It was," said John. "Pioneers traveled here on the way to new settlements. Some gold was even discovered near here."

"I wish I could find gold," said Susan.

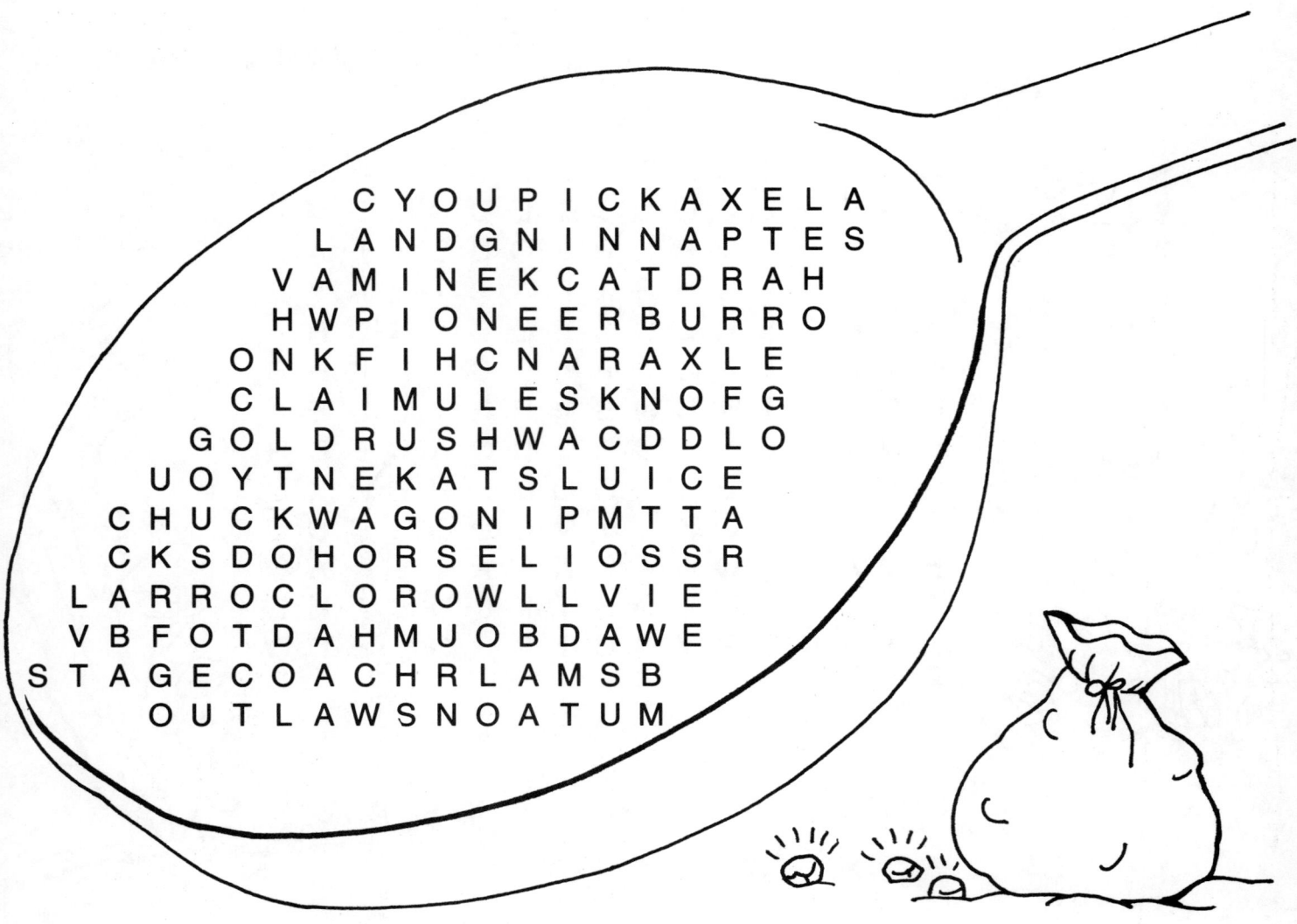

Find and circle everything that has to do with the Old West.

CHUCKWAGON	PIONEER	CORRAL	SLUICE	AXLE	MINE
STAGECOACH	CAMPFIRE	OUTLAW	BURRO	LAND	HORSE
HARDTACK	PANNING	CLAIM	BANDIT	MULE	GOLD
GOLDRUSH	PICKAXE	RANCH	STAKE		

"We can pretend we're pioneers," said John. "Tomorrow morning I'll come back with my nephew. We'll show you how to pan for gold. Western streams still have gold in them."

John stopped suddenly. He bent down and picked something up.

"I think this is a piece of gold. It may be fool's gold, though." He showed the kids a piece of shiny metal.

"It's going to be dark soon," said John. "We'd better hurry."
"I can see the stars already!" said Jerry.
"I know the names of some of them," said Susan. "I like to look at the stars."
They looked up at the sky.

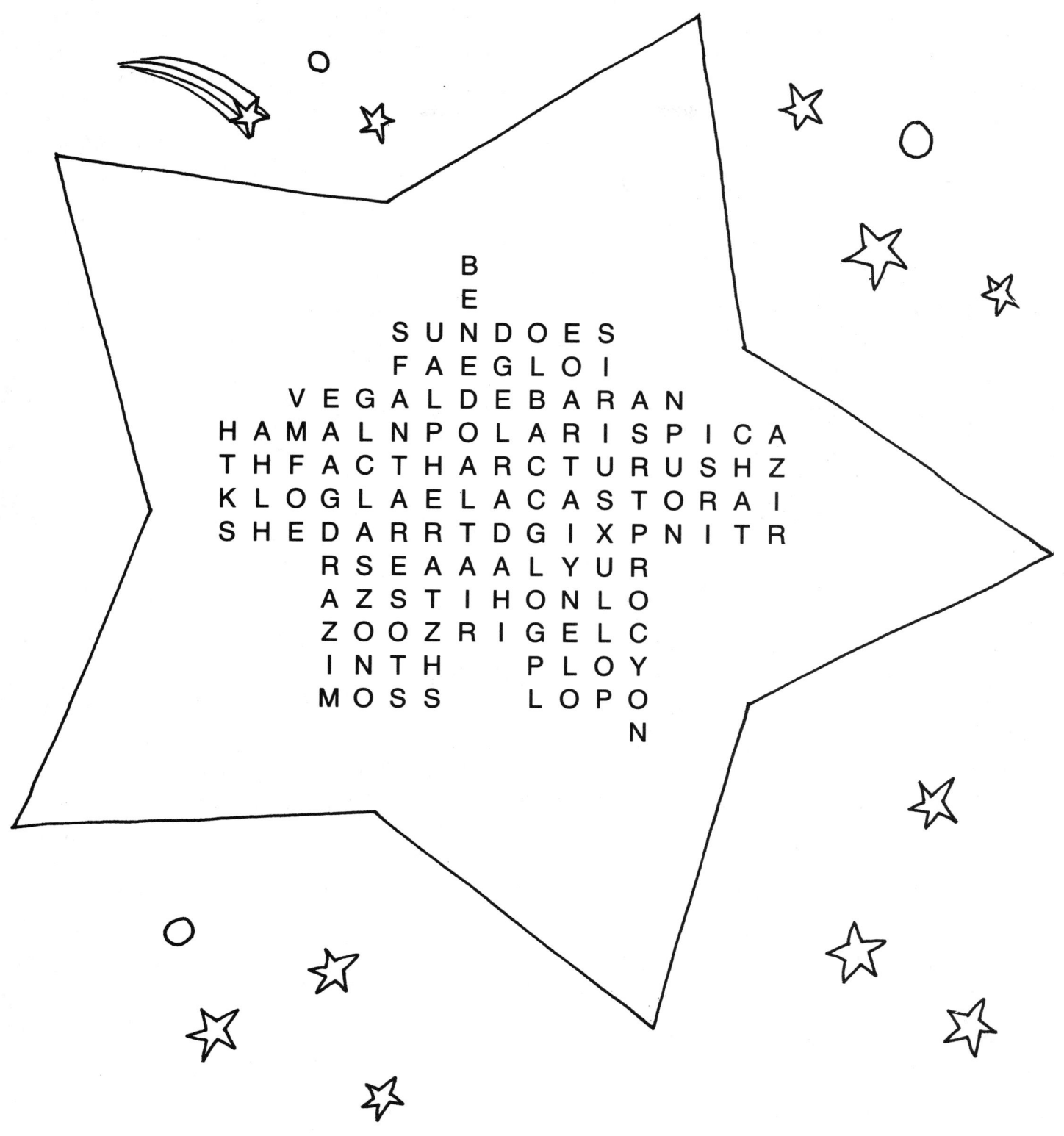

Find and circle the names of stars.

ALDEBARAN	MIZAR	POLARIS	VEGA	ALTAIR	SHEDAR	SUN
ALPHERATZ	RIGEL	ANTARES	ALGOL	POLLUX	CASTOR	HADAR
ARCTURUS	DENEB	PROCYON	SPICA	SIRIUS	HAMAL	

As Jerry and Susan ran into camp, their parents met them.

"We were beginning to get a little worried," said Dad. "We thought you got lost."

"We did," said Susan, "but John found us!" She introduced John to Mom and Dad.

"We found gold! We saw birds and stars and... everything!" shouted Jerry. "And tomorrow we're going to pan for gold! You can come, too!"

44

"Wow!" said Mom. "It sounds like camping turned out okay."
"Please stay for dinner," Dad said to John.
They ate fresh trout, sang campfire songs and toasted marshmallows.
"Tomorrow morning we pan for gold, okay?" Jerry asked Mom and Dad.
"It sure is!" said Mom, laughing.
"Then we can plan our next camping trip!" said Susan.

Find and circle the things that have to do with the family's camping trip.

STREAM	MARSHMALLOW	OUTDOORS	STAR	ANIMAL	FISHING	LAKE
FRIEND	ADVENTURE	CANOEING	SONG	HIKING	ROWING	TENT
INSECT	EXPLORING	VACATION	BIRD	FAMILY		

45

Solutions

Page 4
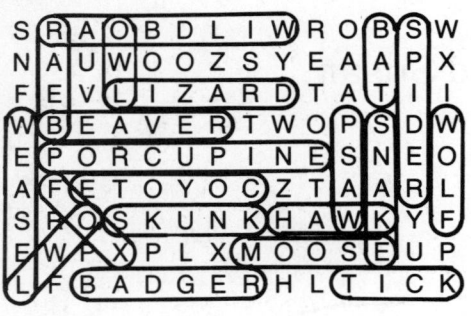

Page 10

Page 6
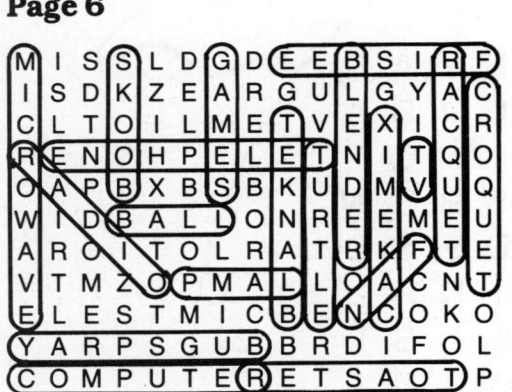

Page 11
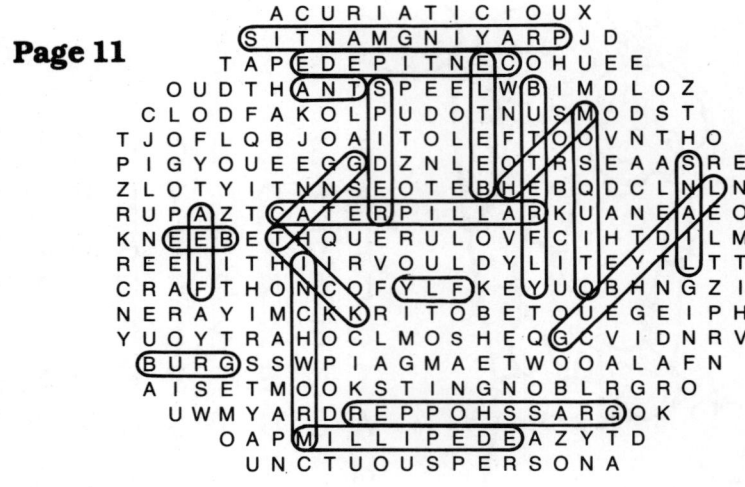

Page 7
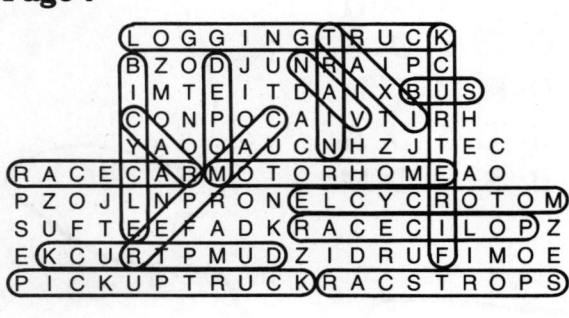

Page 14
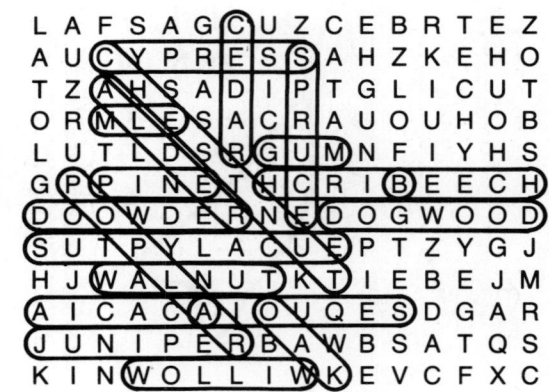

Page 9
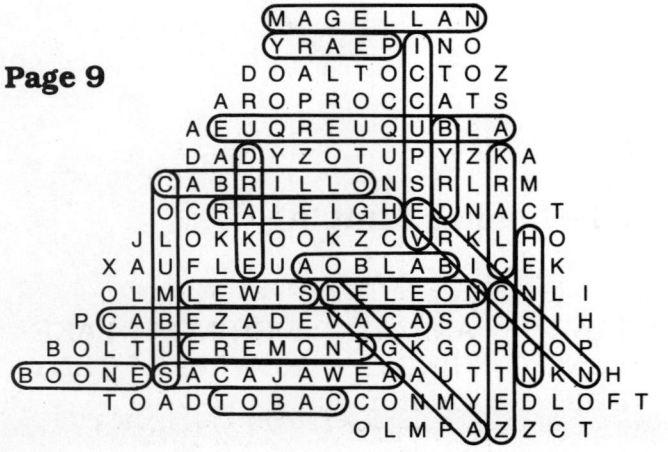

Page 17
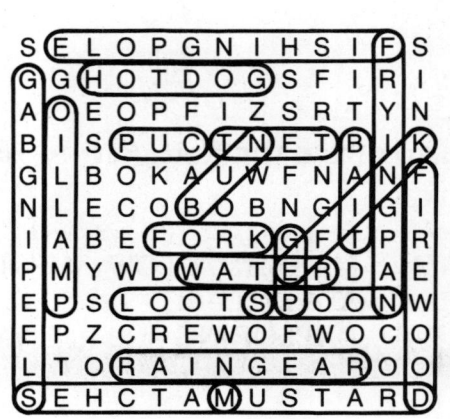

Solutions

Page 19

Page 27

Page 21

Page 30
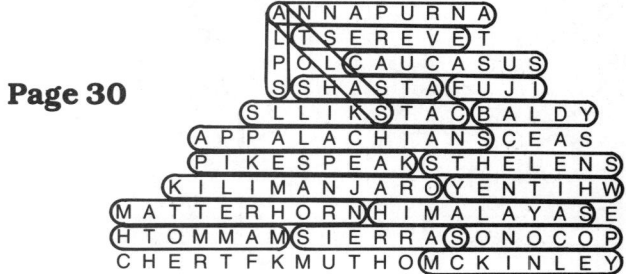

Page 23

Page 31

Page 25

Page 32
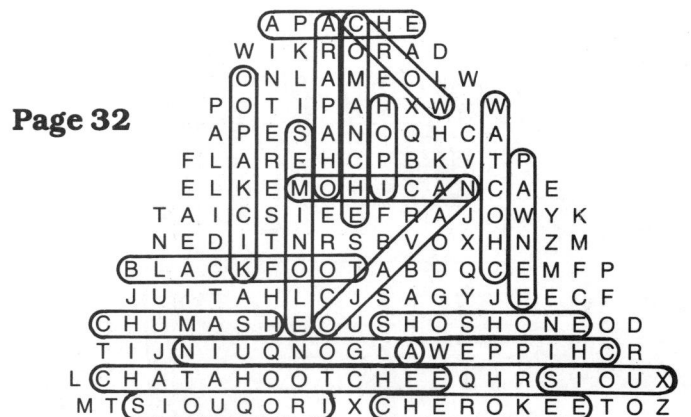

Solutions

Page 34
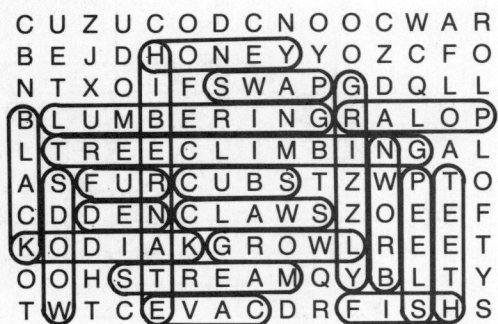

Page 35
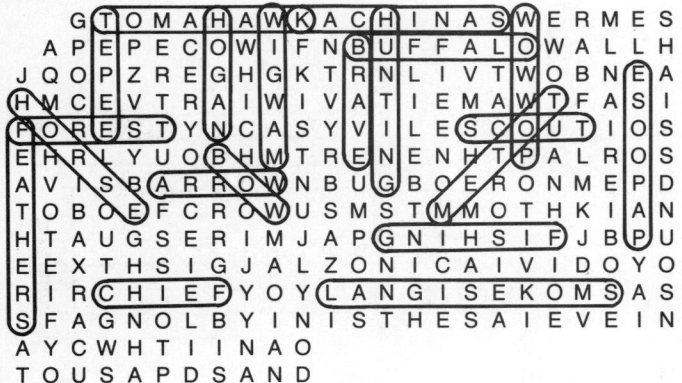

Page 36
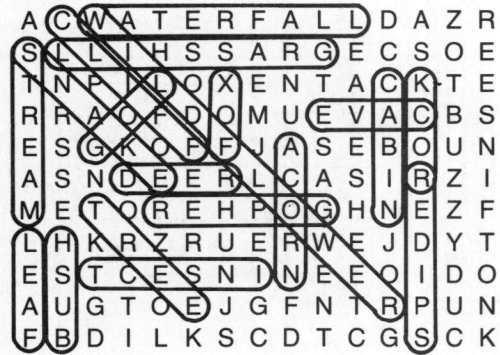

Page 37
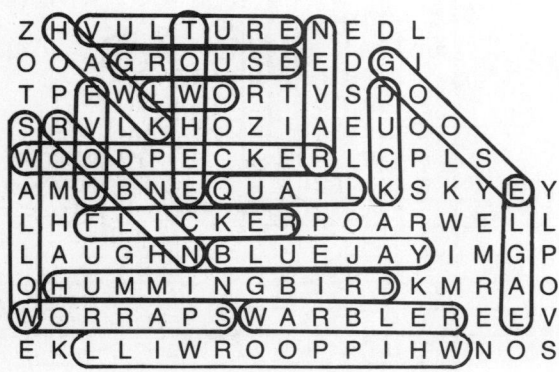

Page 39
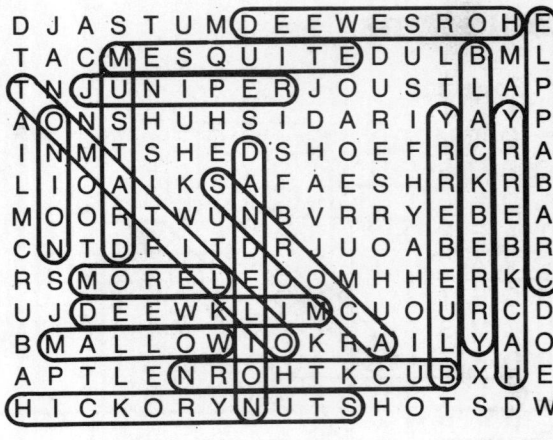

Page 40

Page 43
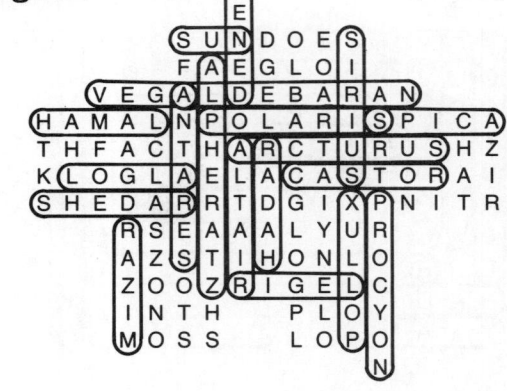

Page 45
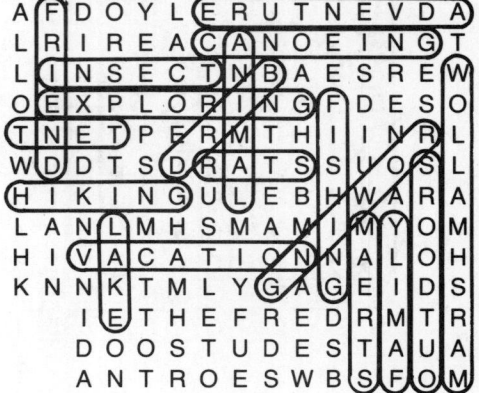